ʼfore

**SCHOOLS
COLLECTION**

TOUGH TIMES
to Be a Kid

THE VIKINGS

Written by
Robin
Twiddy

BookLife
PUBLISHING

©2023
BookLife Publishing Ltd.
King's Lynn, Norfolk
PE30 4LS, UK

A catalogue record for this book is available from the British Library.

ISBN: 978-1-80155-850-1

Written by:
Robin Twiddy
Edited by:
Hermione Redshaw
Designed by:
Danielle Rippengill & Drue Rintoul
Illustrated by:
Amy Li

CONTENTS

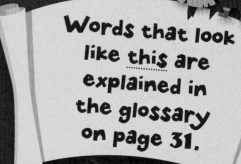

Words that look like this are explained in the glossary on page 31.

It's pretty tough being a kid. Bedtime is never late enough, big brothers hog the TV and there is always someone in the bathroom when you want to go. Well, trust me, it could be worse!

TOUGH LUCK, IT'S MY TURN!

Imagine a world where you are so tired that you are begging for an early bedtime, where there is no TV to watch, just your weird uncle singing a song about how brilliant he is. Worse than all that, imagine a world where there is no bathroom! Well, you just imagined what it's like to be a Viking kid.

I am so great I once jumped over a gate... no hands...

If you think it is tough being a kid today, then strap in. The time of the Vikings is waiting for you, and it is tougher than you can imagine. Don't be fooled by the cool helmets. Being a Viking wasn't all adventure.

THE VIKINGS

It's Viking Time!

Get ready. We are going back in time. You are about to find out what life for a child in Viking times was really like.

The VIKINGS

Now, hold up. Before you get too excited about those cool horned helmets and raiding villages, we should figure out what we mean by Viking. What we call the Vikings were actually a group of people who lived in what we now call Scandinavia from around 800 AD to 1050 AD.

What do you mean I'm not historically accurate?

Let's get something straight. Vikings didn't wear helmets with horns on them. That's just in the movies. The people that we call Vikings didn't call themselves Vikings, either. Well, not all of them. They were actually known as Norsemen. Only the Norse who went on raids were known as Vikings.

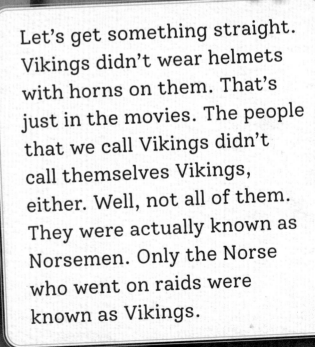

Vikings were known as great <u>sailors</u>. They would travel around <u>Europe</u> in their boats, attacking <u>settlements</u> by surprise. They were also traders who would buy and sell things from all over during their travels.

Oh no, it's Vikings again! I never know if they are going to pay me or just take everything.

At sea, they were great sailors and soldiers, but at home, they were farmers and fishermen. They weren't one big group of people. They were lots of little groups called clans. These clans sometimes worked together. Other times, they fought each other.

Hey, Erik, are you bored of all this farming yet?

Yeah, Arne, we should find some silly Englishmen to rob.

I like farming. Never lost my sword in a field. Lost one in an Englishman though.

SURVIVING
the Time

If you want to be a Viking, you are going to need to survive being a baby. That's easier said than done. Only eight out of ten Viking children made it to five years old. Eek! It was very important for Vikings to be strong. Babies that the Vikings thought wouldn't be strong might have been left outside on their own.

I'm strong, Dad. Honest!

We don't have to worry about getting sick so much these days. We have doctors, hospitals and years of science-based medicine to help us. Not so for Viking kids. There might have been someone in your Viking village who did medicine. However, they did medicine with a twist. A magical twist.

Is this your kidney?

Not that kind of magic

THE SINGING CURE

If you got sick, an early Viking might just try to cure you with a song or some nice <u>poetry</u>. This was a magical <u>ritual</u> that would try to scare away bad <u>spirits</u> or get the <u>gods</u> on your side.

I know there is a poem in one of these that will cure you.

Vikings didn't use much writing, but they did use a set of <u>symbols</u> called runes. These were thought to be very powerful. Runes carved into stones were sometimes used to try to cure people, too. Check your spelling, though! An old story tells of someone using the wrong rune and making their patient even worse!

Runes

Time out, we actually used some <u>herbs</u>, too. They might have been a bit more helpful than the songs.

MY FATHER'S SON
and My Mother's Daughter

Vikings had very close families. Many generations of Vikings would often live in the same house. Don't worry, most Vikings didn't live too long. There wouldn't be many who lived past thirty-five or forty years of age.

I'm only 17 years old. It's pretty tough being a Viking.

Oh no, my dad's name is Poi...

Vikings didn't have surnames. They would take their father's name and add the Norse for son or daughter to the end. So, if you were a boy and your dad's name was Erik, your name might end up being Erikson.

There might be between 10 and 20 people living in your family home. That's not to mention all the pets. Vikings might have kept cats, dogs, falcons, peacocks and even bears as pets.

Viking children were mostly just considered little adults. Everyone had to help out running the farm. This was especially true when Dad was off with his friends on a raid! He could be gone for weeks, months or maybe forever.

LONG-HOME

Viking homes were called longhouses. That sounds great if you have a big family like the Vikings did. Right? Wrong. It was only one room. Well, the Vikings did usually break it up into three smaller rooms using pillars.

Great, three rooms. But there are 15 of us living here.

Now, don't get too excited about those three rooms yet. One would be used for your farm animals. Another would be used as a workshop. That leaves... yep, one room for you and the family!

Baaa

GRrrrrrrrrr

Ow. Erik just stood on my toe!

Who is licking my elbow?

Bjorn fell asleep on me!

Mooo

ZZZZZZZZZZZZZZZZZZZZ

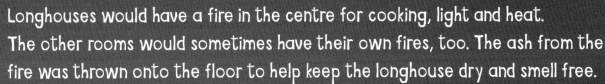

Longhouses would have a fire in the centre for cooking, light and heat. The other rooms would sometimes have their own fires, too. The ash from the fire was thrown onto the floor to help keep the longhouse dry and smell free.

Who's swept up all my carefully placed ash?

Even with the smell of those ashes thrown across the floor, you are not going to get away from the smell of the animals or your family. Life in a longhouse was loud, smelly and maybe a little too cosy.

I never knew Vikings were so smelly!

Stew for Me and
STEW FOR YOU

Vikings ate meat... lots of meat... some more meat... and lots of fish. I hope you aren't a vegetarian, because you are going to have a bad time eating with your Viking family.

It's not easy being a vegetarian Viking.

Vikings did eat vegetables, too, but those vegetables often ended up in a stew with meat. They would keep adding to the same stew pot as they took from it. You might end up with some bits of meat or veg that had been in there for a week or two. Yuck!

I think I have been eating the same stew for the whole winter.

I thought being a Viking was going to be all action. All I have done is farm and cook. I want a FIGHT!

This stew was important for the Vikings. The land they lived on wasn't very good for farming, so they needed to be good at making their food last. As a Viking kid, you would spend a lot of time growing food, preparing food and trying to <u>preserve</u> food.

So much work just for a sandwich!

Just making sure that you had food was hard work as a young Viking. There was no ordering a pizza or nipping down the shop for some butter. You would need to milk the cow or goat, then churn the butter yourself.

Butter lasts longer than milk.

Impressing
THE GODS

I'm watching you!

Gods, gods, gods. The Vikings had a lot of gods. Just like the ancient Greeks, Romans and Egyptians, the Vikings had gods for all sorts of things. Vikings believed that their gods, known as the Aesir, watched over them.

Where most gods were thought to <u>punish</u> wrongdoers and reward those who did good, the Norse gods didn't seem to care about this. They could be impressed or won over through <u>sacrifices</u>, rune magic and <u>prayers</u>.

Is this sandcastle impressive enough for you?

Silly humans. Thor doesn't care what you do unless it is really impressive.

Do you want to hear a poem?

Stories of the gods were handed down through long poems called the Eddas. These told the story of the creation of the universe, how the universe would end and the battles that the Norse gods fought to keep it safe.

Some of the most popular Viking gods were:

Loki was the god of mischief. He was crafty and could not be trusted. His tricks sometimes helped the other gods. Sometimes they helped only Loki.

Odin was the king of the gods. He has one eye. He gave the other away to gain wisdom.

Thor was the god of thunder and strength. Warriors would worship him to become stronger for battles.

oesn't seem wise giving up one of your eyes

I can see that now!

Careful, Thor, you might get thor...I mean sore lifting that hammer.

Nobody ever knows whose side I am on. I will let you in on a secret... It's my side!

Odin

Thor

Loki

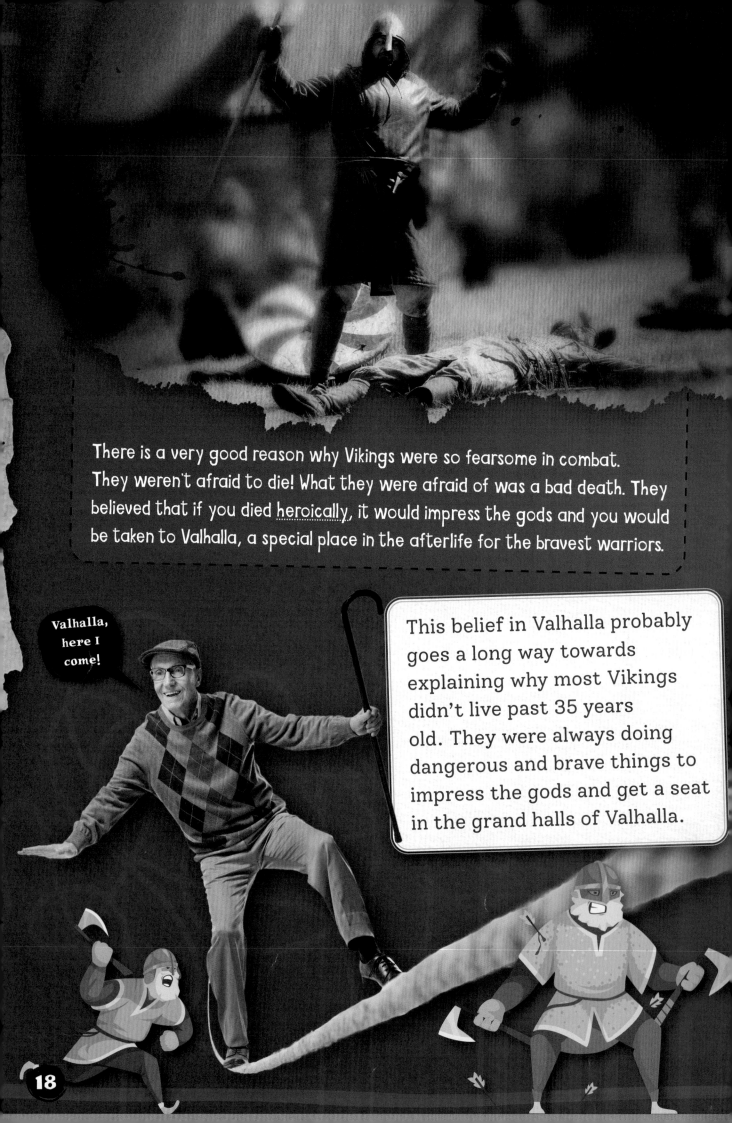

There is a very good reason why Vikings were so fearsome in combat. They weren't afraid to die! What they were afraid of was a bad death. They believed that if you died heroically, it would impress the gods and you would be taken to Valhalla, a special place in the afterlife for the bravest warriors.

Valhalla, here I come!

This belief in Valhalla probably goes a long way towards explaining why most Vikings didn't live past 35 years old. They were always doing dangerous and brave things to impress the gods and get a seat in the grand halls of Valhalla.

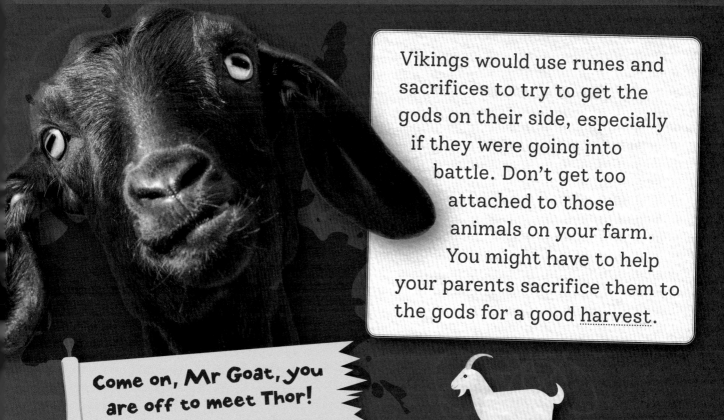

Vikings would use runes and sacrifices to try to get the gods on their side, especially if they were going into battle. Don't get too attached to those animals on your farm. You might have to help your parents sacrifice them to the gods for a good <u>harvest</u>.

Come on, Mr Goat, you are off to meet Thor!

Do you ever feel like the world is ending? Well, the Vikings believed that something called Ragnarök was coming. This was an event that even the gods couldn't stop and would mean the end of everything.

It's tough being a Viking kid, Dad.

Don't worry, Ragnarök is coming. Nothing will be tough after that!

Fashionably FIERCE

I bet you are thinking, oh boy, those Vikings must really stink... Surprisingly, no. Well, maybe a bit. For the time they lived in, they actually bathed quite often. Once a week! Vikings were actually very clean compared to other groups of people who lived at the same time.

Ahhhhhh, it's so nice to get the week's stink off.

Vikings were even known to carry little grooming pouches. Inside, they had tweezers, razors, combs and even ear spoons! Now, you might be wondering what an ear spoon is. An ear spoon is a small spoon used to clean wax out of a Viking's ear.

I wonder if they had a nose spoon?

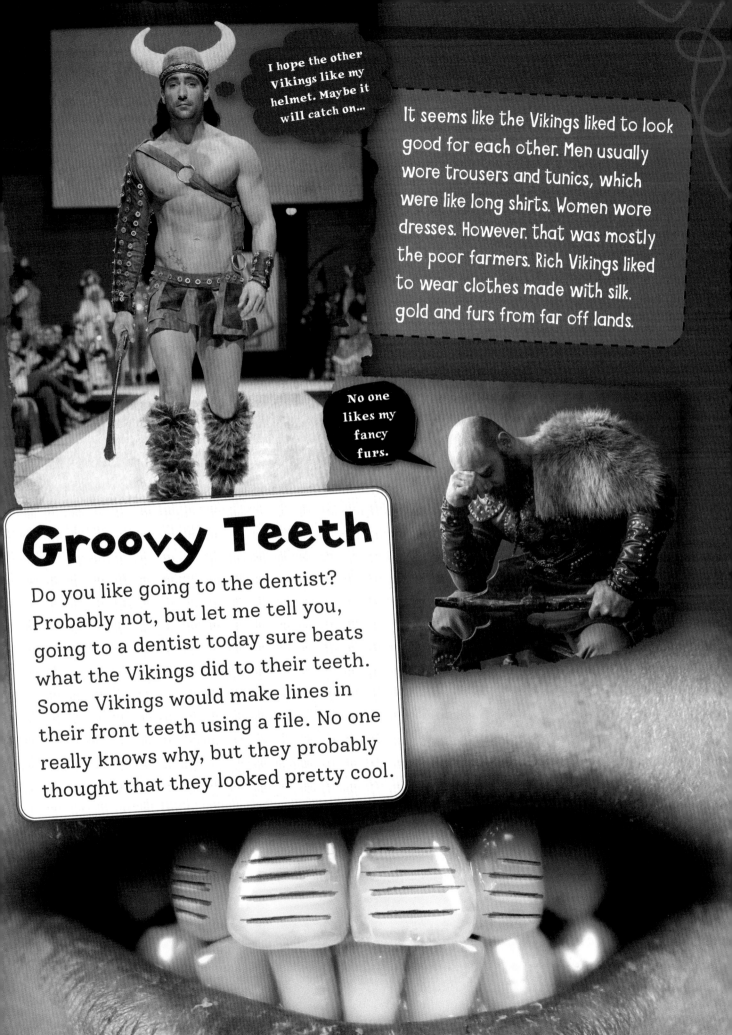

I hope the other Vikings like my helmet. Maybe it will catch on...

It seems like the Vikings liked to look good for each other. Men usually wore trousers and tunics, which were like long shirts. Women wore dresses. However, that was mostly the poor farmers. Rich Vikings liked to wear clothes made with silk, gold and furs from far off lands.

No one likes my fancy furs.

Groovy Teeth

Do you like going to the dentist? Probably not, but let me tell you, going to a dentist today sure beats what the Vikings did to their teeth. Some Vikings would make lines in their front teeth using a file. No one really knows why, but they probably thought that they looked pretty cool.

It's all FUN and GAMES Until...

Are you ready to play, Mr Fluffyson? You are such a cutie.

It was tough as a Viking kid. Even when you were young, you had to work hard to help your family and people who lived around you. However, that did not mean that you didn't get to play. Oh no, quite the opposite. Vikings of all ages loved to play.

Here are some of the fun things that Viking kids could do – when they weren't working on the farm or churning butter. Vikings would go skating on skates made from animal bones. They would also sing, dance and wrestle.

Get ready for some classic Viking fun with a little head wrestling.

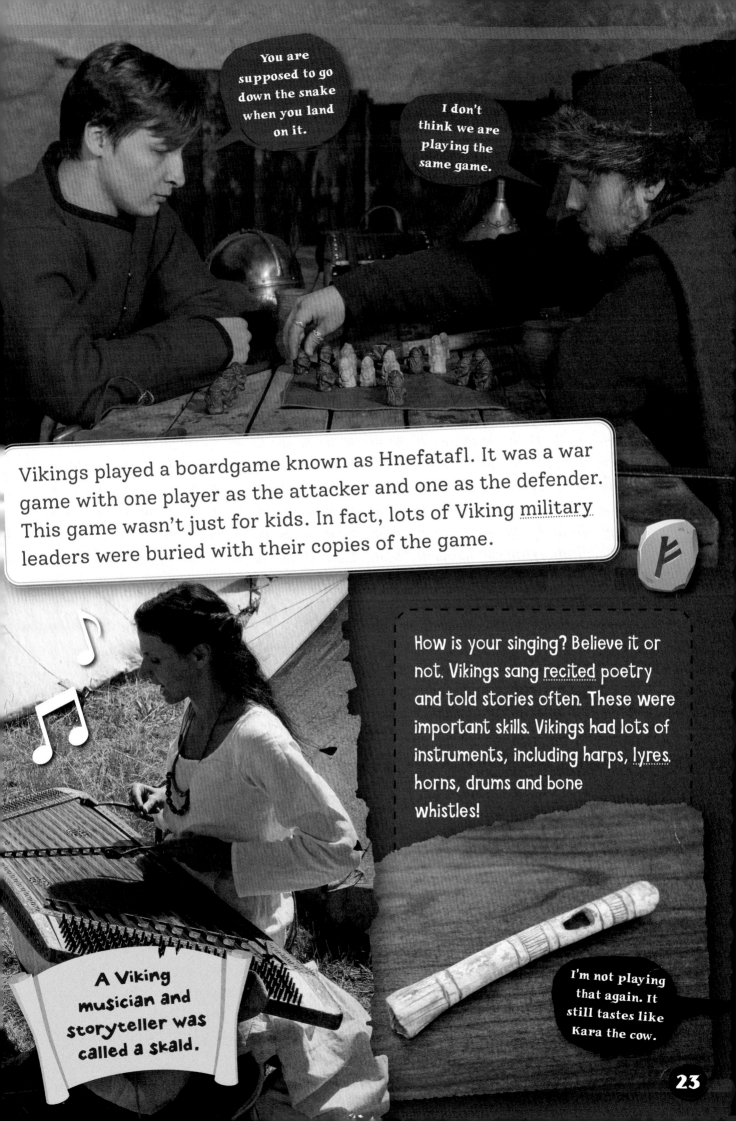

You are supposed to go down the snake when you land on it.

I don't think we are playing the same game.

Vikings played a boardgame known as Hnefatafl. It was a war game with one player as the attacker and one as the defender. This game wasn't just for kids. In fact, lots of Viking <u>military</u> leaders were buried with their copies of the game.

How is your singing? Believe it or not, Vikings sang <u>recited</u> poetry and told stories often. These were important skills. Vikings had lots of instruments, including harps, <u>lyres</u>, horns, drums and bone whistles!

A Viking musician and storyteller was called a skald.

I'm not playing that again. It still tastes like Kara the cow.

There were lots of <u>physical</u> games that Vikings would play to pass the time. Some of these were quite rough. It wasn't unusual for someone to get hurt or even die. One game involved trying to hold your opponent underwater as long as you could. Let's hope you can hold your breath for a long time!

Did I win? Glub... glub...

Vikings would have running races and weightlifting competitions. These were more than just games. These were <u>accomplishments</u>. Winning was something to brag about. A Viking might be asked what his accomplishments were by a king, and they would often describe their sporting achievements to impress him.

I won this trophy for swallowing the most water in the drowning competition.

WETTEST BOY

You might even have some toys as a Viking child. Viking toys weren't as flashy or colourful as they are now. How does a wooden spinning top, wooden sword, bow, toy ship or action figure sound to you? Sounds like fun, but was there something more going on here?

Many toys were actually training tools. Playing with toy swords and ships might seem like a lot of fun until you suddenly have to play with the real thing! That's right, you were training to fight! Even the boardgames were training you to make decisions on the battlefield!

My DADDY Taught Me EVERYTHING I Know

You won't be learning much at Viking school... mostly because there is no such thing. The Vikings didn't really have schools like we have today. Now, you are probably thinking, "brilliant! No school"! Well, slow down. No school doesn't mean no learning.

> Yay, no schoo- Wait, what?

Oh yes, there may not be a school, but there is still plenty to learn as a Viking kid. Since there weren't any Viking teachers, most of your learning would come from Mum and Dad. I hope you like spending time with them... now, you will be working with them, living with them AND learning from them.

> OK, son. The pointy side goes in the other person. Got it?

> Gods, he is here all the time. Can't he just go on a raid or something?

Class, today we will be learning how to make Dad the perfect cup of tea.

You probably want to know what you would be learning, right? Well, do you remember those magic runes the Vikings would write? You would probably learn to read and <u>carve</u> them, but mostly you would learn what your mum and dad did: cooking, sewing and farming.

You would also learn poems, songs and stories. The Vikings had an oral tradition. This means that their history was passed down through stories that were remembered and told to the next generation. You had better have a good memory. Your family history might rely on it!

What was it Uncle Paul did again... slay a dragon? No, he ate a frog. Not sure why we are keeping this story alive.

GROWN UP
at WHAT age?

Remember, Vikings didn't tend to live very long. So, there isn't much time to hang around being a kid. You had better get on with being a Viking.

Cor, Vikings are a lot shorter than I thought.

Feels like only yesterday I was playing with my toys. Oh, it was.

It really was tough being a Viking kid. For the short time that you would get to be a kid, that is. Most of your childhood was spent helping out and working, then bam... you turn 16 and you're a man! Of course, if you were a girl, it was 12 and you were a woman!

Don't think you will get out of going on raids if you are a girl. If you had shown that you were strong and could handle a sword, you would probably be trained to be a shield maiden. Yep, get on the boat. You are off on a raid, too!

Maybe picking up that toy sword wasn't such a good idea!

As a Viking kid, you were really just a little adult in the eyes of your parents. It is just a matter of time until you are strong enough to do more than help on the farm and do chores. Then, that's it... you are a Viking now!

That's TOUGH!

So, you thought it was tough being a kid now. Thank the many Norse gods that you didn't have to grow up in a Viking village. With all that poetry, sharing your home with animals and all the farming, it was pretty tough being a kid in the Viking age.

Phew!

Lucky for you, you won't need to go on any raids or impress the gods with your bravery. Just relax back into your own time and remember, it's not so bad being a kid now. It could be tougher!

What part of being a Viking would be the toughest for you?

GLOSSARY

accomplishments	difficult things that someone has done
AD	after the birth of Jesus, which is used as the starting point for many calendars around the world
carve	to form, shape or write by cutting
creation	the making of something
Europe	the continent that is between Asia and the Atlantic Ocean
generations	groups of people who were born around the same time
gods	beings that are worshiped for having special powers beyond those of nature
harvest	the collection of crops such as grain
herbs	plants that can be used for food, medicine or their smell
heroically	to do things in the way that a hero would, such as being good, honest and brave
lyres	stringed musical instruments much like a harp
medicine	drugs, plants and knowledge used to treat illnesses
military	a country's army and the things that relate to it
mischief	bad behaviour that is often playful but can be dangerous or annoying to others
physical	to do with the body or movement
pillars	tall cylinders that are used to support a structure
poetry	a spoken or written set of words that use rhythm
prayers	the act of asking a god or gods for something
preserve	to be kept in good condition
punish	to cause suffering or pain for doing something wrong
raiding	attacking quickly to steal
recited	to speak aloud something remembered
ritual	a set of actions or steps done in a special way during a religious ceremony
sacrifices	to give something precious, often the life of an animal, to a god or gods
sailors	people who work on boats at sea
settlements	where a group of people have moved to and started a home, often where there were no homes before
spirits	beings that are not part of this world, such as a ghost or devils
symbols	something that stands in for another thing
wisdom	good judgement and understanding
worship	love and devotion shown to an object, person or god

INDEX

Photo Credits
All images are courtesy of Shutterstock.com, unless otherwise specified. With thanks to Getty Images, Thinkstock Photo and iStockphoto.

Recurring images – YamabikaY, Tartila, TADDEUS, sumkinn, Vlada Young, Gaidamashchuk, pics five, adecvatman , Sabelskaya, dimethylorange, Andrey_Kuzmin. Cover – Danny Smythe, David Persson, Helga Miller. 2–3 – Prystai. 4–5 – Roman Samborskyi, ANURAK PONGPATIMET, Malchev, Obsidian Fantasy Studio, Prostock-studio, Sakura Image Inc. 6–7 – Alan Kean, Artindo, Drevs, Krakenimages.com, Marjolein Hameleers. 8–9 – Elnur, Inara Prusakova, Krakenimages.com, Ljupco Smokovski, Olga Turovskaja Olga Turovskaja, On Lollipops. 10–11 – Dreams Come True, Krakenimages.com, Lunapi, Natalya Fedotova, summer studio. 12–13 – Anna Krivitskaya, Ben Gingell, Irina Bortmann, Mary Long, TTphoto, Volha Werasen. 14–15 – Anna Krivitskaya, Elena Sherengovskaya, Human Being Studio, Jemastock. 16–17 – aleksandr_pa_vector, Drakuliren, Alexander Sviridov, HSBortecin, Tomacco, Tribalium. 18–19 – Roman Evgenev, Ljupco Smokovski, Anna Kucherova, Elena Sherengovskaya, Panda Vector, BNP Design Studio, klyaksun, Macrovector. 20–21 – criben, kwanchai.c, Nomad_Soul, Vital9s. 22–23 – FXQuadro, Venghaul, Zyabich, Kyle Wiles. 24–25 – Belight, Krakenimages.com, Daxiao Productions, Claudia Harms-Warlies. 26–27 – nakaridore, NataliAlba, Viktor Osipenko, Bernardo Emanuelle. 28–29 – Maria Madrinan, Chubykin Arkady, Chris Cornish. 30–31 – Bob Hilscher, ANURAK PONGPATIMET.